IMAGES
of America

BURLINGTON

VOLUME II

IMAGES
of America

BURLINGTON
VOLUME II

Mary Ann DiSpirito
and David Robinson

ARCADIA
PUBLISHING

Cover Photograph: Eleven miles of trolley line extended throughout Burlington in the first decade of this century, connecting Rock Point, Queen City Park, Winooski, Colchester, and Essex Junction with downtown and the waterfront. Elias Lyman was president of the company, and W.F. Hendee was the secretary and treasurer. (UVM.)

CONTENTS

Acknowledgments   6

Introduction   7

1.   On the Waterfront   9

2.   Church Street   21

3.   Downtown   31

4.   Street Scenes   41

5.   Enterprises   53

6.   Celebrating Champlain   65

7.   Happenings   73

8.   The Moody Winooski   81

9.   School Days   87

10.   On the Hill   99

11.   Community Medicine   109

12.   Neighboring Faiths   117

ACKNOWLEDGMENTS

We wish to thank Louis DiSpirito, Felicia Robinson, Ellen and Jeffrey Vande Griek for their good-natured encouragement, patience, and support during our months of work on this book, and Miss Jean Read for her wonderful memories. We also are grateful to the following sources and contributors, whose images have made this collection possible:

The Burlington Department of Public Works, Water Division – Thomas M. Dion, CPO
The John Barrows and Sarah Carpenter Collection – Sanborn Insurance Maps
Richard J. Derry – The Lake Champlain Reef Runners
Louis DiSpirito
Fletcher Allen Health Care, Compliments of the Public Relations Department – Photographs Taken
   by Dr. H.A. Durfee, Dr. K.F. Truax, L.L. McAllister, and Harry Stevens
The Fletcher Free Library – Amber Collins, Co-director
The Gerald B. Fox Collection – Photographs of the Railroad and Waterfront
Sylvia Heininger Holden – The Erna Heininger Family Album
The Alfred Holden Collection
The Lake Champlain Transportation Company – Photographs of Lake Transportation
Rita Lefebvre – The Stable Interior
Annabelle Pinkham Miller, Miss Vermont 1954
Jeanne Carter Miller – The Val Carter Album
North Country Books, Burlington, VT, Mark Ciufo and Joel Dumas
The Ohavi Zedek Synagogue and the Black Family
The Archives of the Roman Catholic Diocese of Burlington
Special Collections, University of Vermont (UVM)
Trinity College of the Vermont/Sisters of Mercy
Doug Tucker – UVM Training Regiment
Rebecca Turner – The Hazel Miner Family Album, the 1927 Flood, and the Sears Building Fire

We also acknowledge our debt for information provided by Burlington annual reports and city directories; Charles Allen's *About Burlington Vermont* (1905), from which some images were drawn; issues of *The Burlington Free Press* from 1858 through 1959; *Illustrated Burlington, Vt.* (1906); Luther B. Johnson's *Vermont in Floodtime* (1928); John T. Cushing's and Arthur F. Stone's (Eds) *Vermont in the World War: 1917 to 1919* (1928); Arthur F. Stone's *Vermont of Today* (1929, three volumes); Elin Anderson's *We Americans* (1937); Lilian Baker Carlisle's, Margaret Muller's, David Blow's, and Samuel Hatfield's *Look Around Burlington, Vermont* (1972); Steven Roth's *History of Trinity College, 1925–1975* (1975); Peter Carlough's *Bygone Burlington* (1977); Ralph Nading Hill's "Two Centuries of Ferry Boating on Lake Champlain," in *Lake Champlain Ferryboats*, published by the Lake Champlain Transportation Company (1990); David Blow's and Lilian Baker Carlisle's *Historic Guide to Burlington Neighborhoods, Vol's I and II* (1991, 1997); and Robert Michaud's *Salute to Burlington* (1991).

INTRODUCTION

In 1609, Samuel de Champlain and his men were the first Europeans to view what is now Burlington. Three hundred years later his discovery and the subsequent naming of the lake were commemorated by this city in a lavish celebration, which lasted several days. During these 300 years, Burlington evolved from a wilderness into a small settlement and eventually into the largest city in Vermont.

Incorporated by settlers of English descent in 1763, the town's proximity to the lake, combined with the determination of its founders, quickly attracted inhabitants and commerce to the area. Ira Allen surveyed Burlington in 1772 and, in 1773, Ethan, Heman, Zimri, and Ira Allen formed the Onion River Land Company, which comprised 300,000 acres and included land owned by Edward Burling of White Plains, New York. The town's population declined during the Revolutionary War, when 40 families evacuated to escape the path of the British Army as it moved down Lake Champlain toward battlegrounds at Hubbardton, Bennington, and Saratoga.

After the war, in 1783, Stephen Lawrence was the first to return with his family. The first store was established in 1789; that same year, Frederick Saxton built the first frame house at the head of Pearl Street. By 1791, the first official census counted 332 residents. The town of Burlington was then considered large enough to sustain a post office, which opened in 1792.

The rise of the lumber industry and the use of ships for transport established the waterfront area as the early center of commerce. To be close to the people he treated, Dr. John Pomeroy built the first brick house in 1797 at what is now 164 Battery Street. The structure held his offices as well as his residence; the practice of combining work and home was common to professional men at that time. It is noteworthy that in 1797, both Essex and Hinesburg were larger than Burlington, and Charlotte had twice as many inhabitants.

John H. Johnson made the first official survey map of the town in March 1836. The 1840 census showed 4,271 residents, a number that surpassed 7,500 by the end of the decade. Burlington was incorporated as a city in 1865; by 1870, the population reached 14,387. Burlingtonians of the era enjoyed "modern conveniences," such as natural gas for heating and lighting, a water works and sewer system, daily newspapers, and other amenities of comfortable living.

Burlington's beauty, as well as a determined promotional campaign by Ira Allen, made it a natural location for the University of Vermont, which the state legislature chartered in 1791. In time, other institutions of higher learning were also attracted to the Queen City and its environs. The founding and growth of Trinity College, Champlain College, Burlington College, the Community College of Vermont in Burlington, and nearby St. Michael's College profoundly shaped the character of Burlington.

Besides businessmen and promoters, educators, doctors, ministers, and statesmen also played their roles in shaping the city's culture. As a result, libraries, theaters, an opera house, many churches, and social services have all combined to provide a quality of life Burlingtonians enjoy.

Early images of Burlington were sketches and engravings, several of which appear in this book. The advent of photography before the Civil War encouraged many residents to record public and private scenes of city life. These are the images we have included. As in our first volume, we again selected some photographs for their historical value, even when the images were imperfect.

We are grateful to the private collectors who have allowed their photographs to be used; some of these images are being published for the first time. Searching through their family albums, storage boxes, and archives became a treasure hunt that yielded many prizes.

This second volume again covers the century from 1860 to 1960, when black-and-white photography flourished. We are pleased to include many striking images that capture landmarks, city streets, daily life, and historic high points in this small city of neighbors and friends.

We hope those Burlingtonians who read this book will gain a better understanding and enjoyment of their city's history and the daily lives of those who went before us. For those readers who are not fortunate enough to live in Burlington, we offer in this book a glimpse of the people, scenery, and events that have molded this small city into the unique community it is today.

Mary Ann DiSpirito
David Robinson
Burlington, Vermont
March 1999

One

ON THE WATERFRONT

Visitors arriving in Burlington via the lake were impressed by the view and by the city's prosperity. Burlington had grown from a few rough dwellings in the 1760s to a true metropolis by 1840. Placed on the breakwater by a steamboat company, the lantern in the foreground tended to blow out during storms. Nevertheless, it remained in service until 1865.

By the 1850s, the railroad proved to be the most economical way to transfer freight. Local entrepreneurs welcomed the opportunity, and by the 1880s, commerce thrived because of their foresight. The roundhouse and the maze of tracks shown were located south of Maple Street.

As the nation's third-largest lumber port in 1873, Burlington's lumberyards were so extensive that the paths between the stacks were given street names. In 1889, the wholesale lumber trade boasted capital of $2,158,000 and annual sales of $3,475,000. Wages paid to 955 employees totaled $26,790 each month.

The proximity of the tracks, lumberyards, and manufacturing to lake travel enhanced Burlington's commercial position. Battery Park offered a view of trains and steamboats bringing passengers and freight from all over the world. Caught during a quiet moment around the time of the Civil War, the yards were soon teeming with activity.

A "great fire" swept through the Pioneer Shops on June 6, 1888. Consisting of four separate buildings built c. 1860, the shops provided incubator space for manufacturers. One such firm was founded by E.W. Chase and Lyman E. Smith. Chase & Smith manufactured sash doors, blinds, and stairs; the company employed 30 men and did $25,090 in business in 1865.

Erected at the foot of College Street by Central Vermont Railroad in 1861, the depot was used by both the Rutland and Central Vermont Railroads. Improvements in the manufacture of tracks and cars brought safety and comfort, increasing the number of travelers. Locomotives introduced in 1882 could attain a speed of 70 miles per hour.

By 1906, local businessmen and residents were aware that Union Station was aging and too small for the amount of passenger traffic coursing through it daily. The business community appointed a "Committee of Fifteen" to negotiate with the railroads; this process lasted several years.

The city of Burlington donated land at the foot of College Street and contributed $15,000 to build the new depot and reroute the tracks; the railroad company paid a total of $130,000 for the construction. The new Union Station opened in 1915 and remained a hub of activity for several decades. The building is now owned by the Main Street Landing Company.

In 1894, the city transferred the water intake from the harbor area to, as the water department stated in its annual report, a "more healthful position in the more frequently agitated waters of the broad lake." Working from a scow, divers connected the 75-foot sections of pipe.

This young man's responsibility was to melt the lead used for attaching the Falcon ball joints that connected the pipes. The joints were then covered with special latex to render them watertight. Unknown then to be a health hazard, the task of melting lead was often assigned to boys.

This view of the scow shows the enormous 2-foot diameter sections of iron pipe. Two miles of the pipe were laid, costing the city $47,239.46. Water Commissioners Henry Greene, W.E. Hall, and J.E. Lanou stated that the money was well spent, as "many detect an improvement in quality."

The intake pipe was located in about 30 feet of water on Appletree Reef. The highest point of the copper screen that capped the conduit stood approximately 14 feet below the surface when the water was low. The location proved to be too shallow and the pipe was eventually shortened to Rock Point, where it now serves as a stand-by intake. The old line did not have the ability to control zebra muscles, which were introduced by vessels from the Greal Lakes. A new line capable of dealing with the non-native bivalves was laid during the early 1980s, when the filter plant was upgraded.

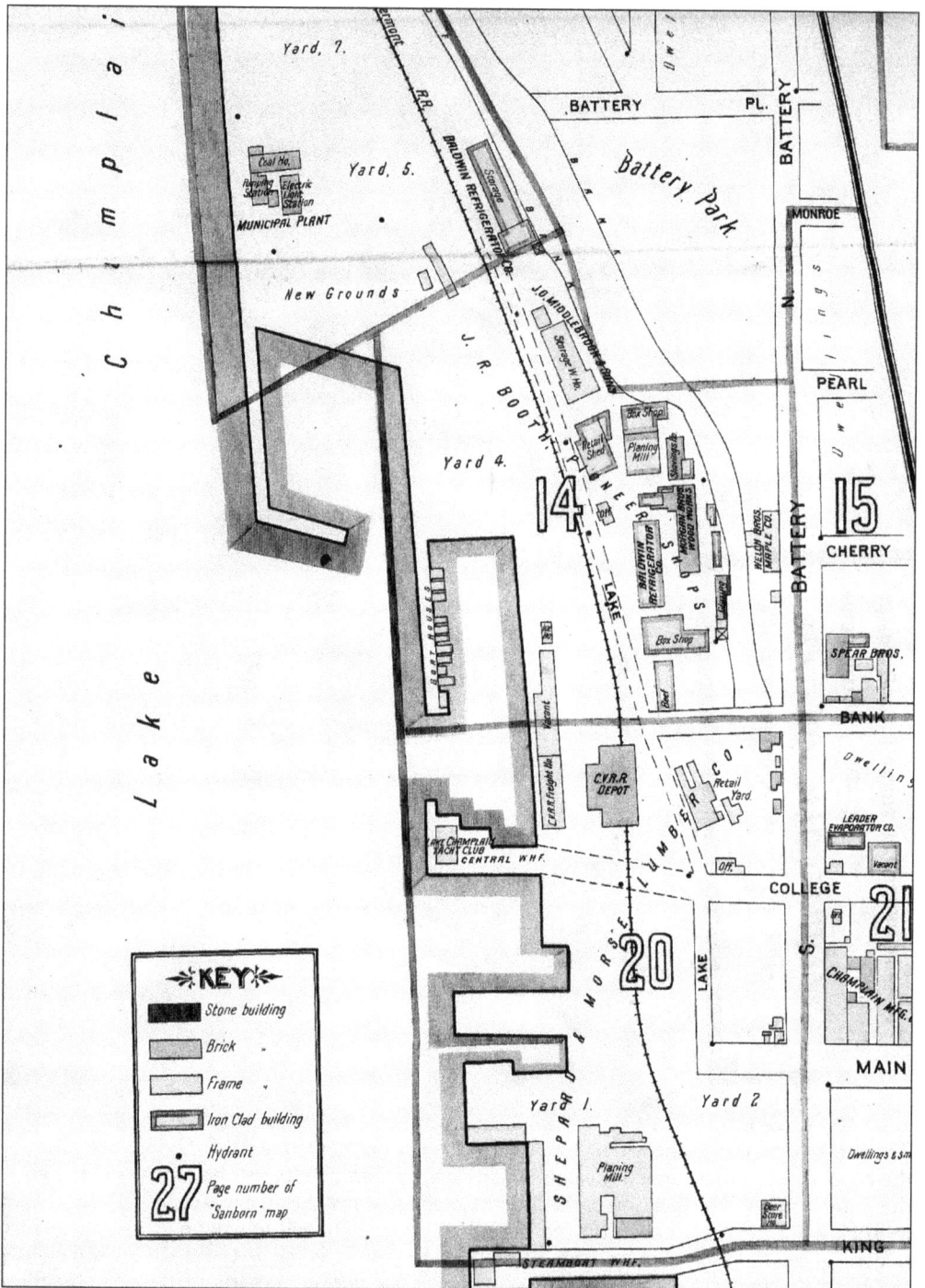

As shown in this 1906 Sanborn Insurance map, lumber milling and manufacturing still dominated the waterfront at the turn of the century. J.R. Booth, a Canadian, purchased the Pioneer shops in 1878 from E.W. Chase's estate; he rebuilt them after the 1888 fire. The Leader Evaporator Company on Battery Street made evaporators used in the process of making maple sugar.

This copper screen caps the intake pipe shown on p. 15. Zebra mussels form colonies upon these screens, which eventually disrupt the flow of water

The waterfront was a hub of activity during the 1909 tercentenary celebration of the founding of Lake Champlain. Union Station is located on the right and the yacht club can be seen to the left of center. The bleachers on the left provided seating for the pageants. (UVM.)

In 1938, war erupted again in Europe, and although the United States was not yet involved, troops remained ready. As a part of the cavalry, this horse-drawn artillery unit was preparing to board the *Ticonderoga* on its way to training exercises.

By the 1940s, signs of decay permeated the waterfront. Green Mountain Power occupied most of Union Station in 1940 as passenger rail traffic declined. A railroad strike, which affected the Rutland Railroad, ended passenger service in 1953. (UVM.)

18

The Champlain ferry docks were inundated in 1942. Built in the 1870s by the Champlain Transportation Company (the world's oldest steamboat company and the forerunner of the Lake Champlain Transportation Company), the structure was replaced by a snack bar and gift shop in 1961. (UVM.)

The Lake Champlain Reef Runners Skin Diving Club introduced scuba diving to Lake Champlain during the 1950s. In this 1959 photograph, Club Vice President Jerry Donovan is about to make the first dive beneath the ice in Burlington Harbor. Past Club President Dick Derry assists Jerry Donovan with the dive.

On October 2, 1958, the Reef Runners outfitted a duck amphibious vehicle (DUKW) as Civil Defense Director Lionel Loveday (foreground) exchanged information with Squadron Chairman Harold Simpers. The club became a disaster squad operation as part of the local civil defense, performing rescues and retrieving drowning victims.

Two

CHURCH STREET

Rowe's Hotel was located on the northwest corner of Church and Cherry Streets during the Civil War. Originally the Stanton House, Rowe purchased the hotel from his father-in-law, Henry Stanton, in 1864. A popular meeting place, Rowe's later became the Sherwood Hotel. A dog sits on the stairs that were used to descend from carriages. (UVM.)

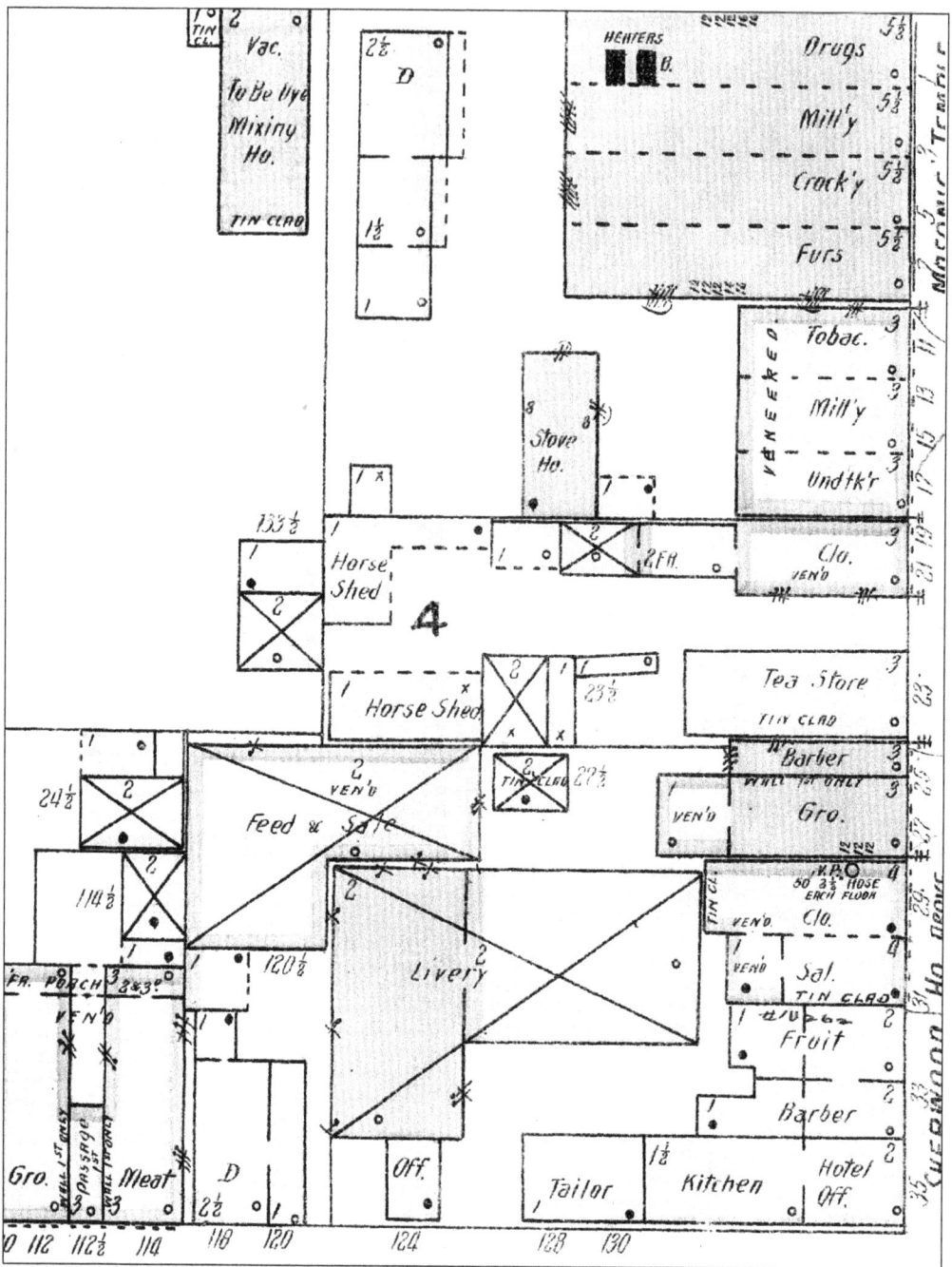

Church Street quickly took over as the center of commerce during the decline of the waterfront. Shoppers on upper Church Street had a variety of stores from which to choose. Mrs. P.H. McMahon ran the millinery shop on the first floor of the Masonic Temple. The Union Pacific Tea Company was located at 23 Church Street. The Sherwood Hotel dominated the corner. Note the livery stables and horse sheds.

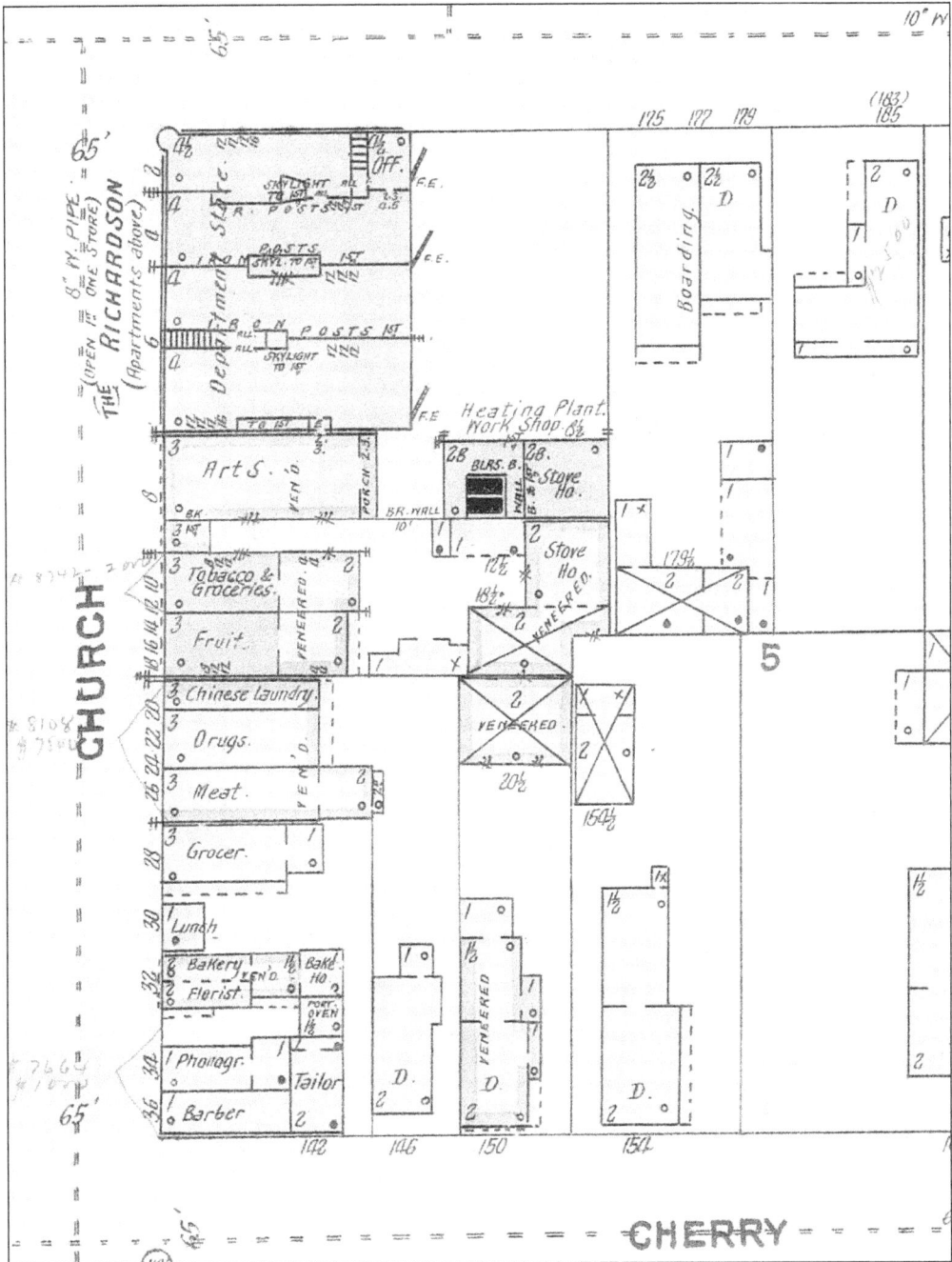

The Richardson Apartments were considered "palatial"; the H.W. Allen & Company occupied the lower floors. Owned by Heman W. Allen and his associate F.D. Abernethy, the business was established in 1844. The building is now known as Richardson Place. Charlie Sing operated the Chinese laundry at 26 Church; Raine and Burt were "dealers in fancy groceries" at 28 Church.

By the mid-1920s, Charlie Sing had moved his laundry to Cherry Street. Looking down Cherry Street toward the intersection of Church, the penthouse on the New Sherwood Hotel is visible; a portion of the People's Store can also be seen across the street. (UVM.)

The next two decades saw even more dramatic changes on upper Church Street. Preston's was now a well-established jewelry store and a new Sears Building replaced the structure that had once housed the Sherwood Hotel. The space is now occupied by a Borders bookstore.

24

This postcard of the New Sherwood Hotel does not show the penthouse. T.H. Murphy modernized the building and, in 1906, the hotel had steam heat, electric lights, and a dining room with "superior table service." Rates for the 50 rooms began at $1.50 per night.

Church Street was a bustle of activity during the 1930s. The block shown is between Bank and Cherry Streets. The building on the right that housed the Mayfair Beauty Salon burned during the 1970s. The one-story building with the awning is now the site of Brooks Pharmacy.

The same block during the 1940s shows some changes. Kelley Pharmacy remained in that location until the latter half of the 1990s. Although trolley cars were no longer in use, tracks are still visible in the roadway.

The block between College and Bank Streets shows the Howard Opera House on the left. The first opera performed was Donizetti's *Lucia di Lammermoor*, which opened February 24, 1879. In this image from a souvenir booklet of the 1880s, the hitching posts indicate that horses and carriages were to be tethered on one side of the street.

The Howard Opera House was built *c.* 1878–79 by John Purple Howard. Designed by Vermonter Steven Hatch, the Italian Renaissance edifice cost $100,000. High insurance costs closed the Howard in 1904; the space was converted into shops and offices. Magram's Department Store operated there until the late 1980s.

At the turn of the century, F.L. Taft & Company, druggists, had been operating in Burlington for over 40 years. In addition to pharmaceuticals, Taft was the local agent of Eastman Cameras and Kodak; they carried supplies and provided developing and printing services for amateur photographers.

Photographed by Erna Heininger, the first female dentist in Burlington, the single X marks the window of her office. The double X's show the location of the Kieslich Construction Company. The Central Drug Store occupies the former site of F.L Taft & Company. Leunig's is now in that space.

Built of white marble in 1931, the Chittenden Trust Company Building was purchased by Merchants Bank in 1970. When Merchants Bank moved in the early 1990s, the bank divided the building into offices and retail space. The original lobby and teller floor is now a pub.

This image of the bank lobby documents the opulence of the public area and teller cages. The stairwell at the right led to the vaults and the small balcony allowed bank officers to view their customers. During the Merchants Bank era, the reception area was in the rear just above the three steps.

This c. 1930 photograph, taken looking up Church Street from the corner of Main Street, shows the new city hall. Constructed of Vermont marble, granite, slate, and brick, the building opened to the public on May 12, 1928, when an estimated 12,000 people passed through it. The bell in the cupola is of concert quality and rings in tone E.

Three

DOWNTOWN

A wooden bridge on College Street crosses the ravine that once bisected Burlington. The top of city hall can be seen at the left, the spire of the Baptist church is to the right of center, and a tower of the cathedral is faintly visible on the far right. (UVM.)

An easterly view of College Street from St. Paul, in 1880, shows the area on the left that was rebuilt into the "Bank Block" during the 1890s. B. Turk & Company was a well-known manufacturer of fine clothing and operated an emporium at 156–158 College Street.

In just a few short years, poles bringing telephone and electric services to businesses were becoming more commonplace throughout the city.

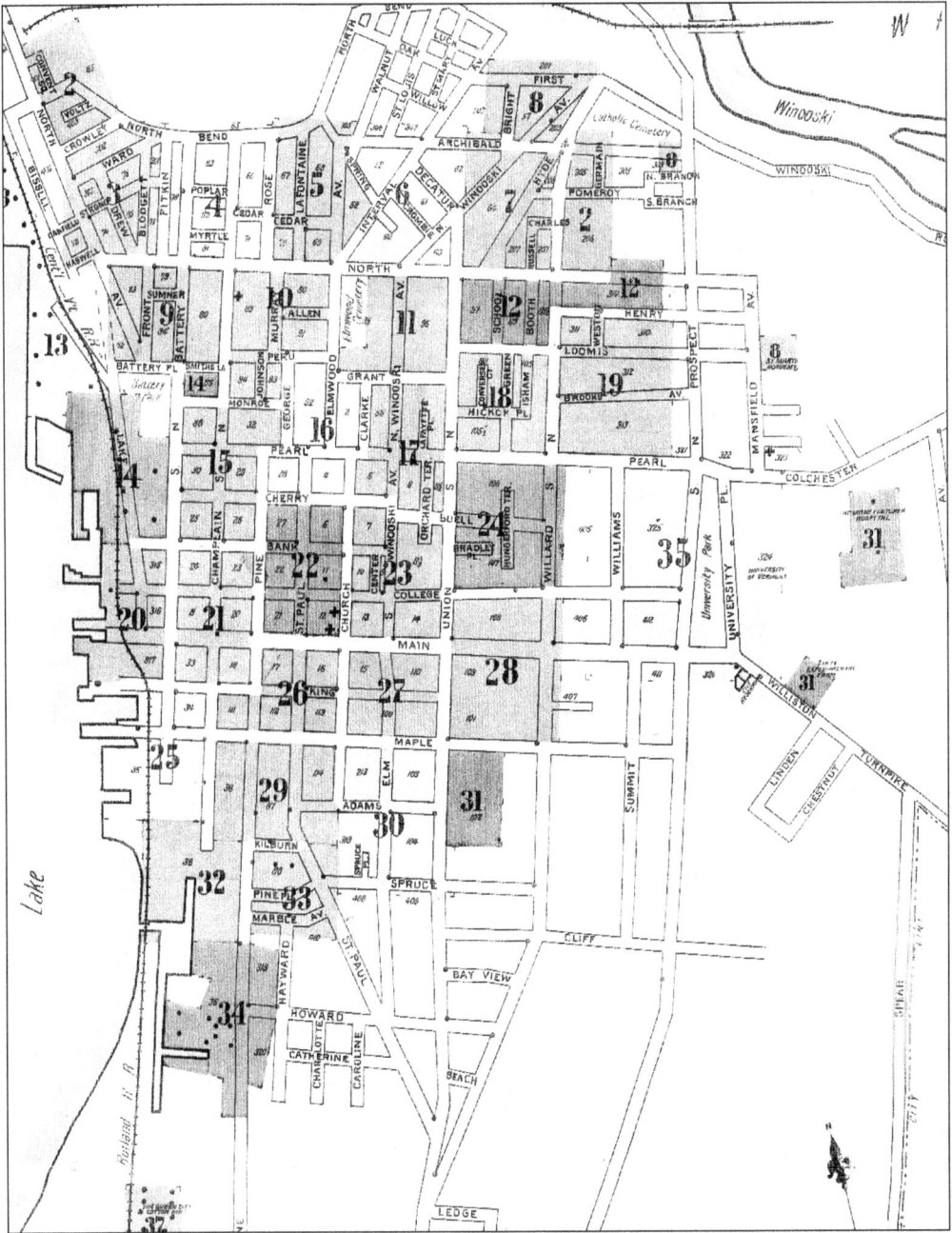

The downtown area, in 1906, contained a mix of businesses in the area surrounded by Main Street, Pine Street, Pearl Street, and South Winooski Avenue, just as it does today. Some street names have been changed over the intervening years.

The Berry-Hall Building at 115–117 College Street was constructed in 1871 by Roby Brothers, architects. Berry, Hall, and Company was the largest coffee and spice mill in New England. The Wells & Richardson Company hired A.B. Fisher to build the structure housing the Burlington Drug Company in this photograph. From 1942 to 1961, the *Burlington Daily News* was located there. The site is presently occupied by Bennington Potters. O.C. Taylor sold pipes and tobacco.

Sidewalks were added to many of Burlington's streets when they were resurfaced during the 1920s. This crew is spreading asphalt on Center Street, with the steamroller waiting to tamp the surface. The photograph was taken looking toward Bank Street; a parking garage has now replaced the mansard-roofed building to the right of center.

Horse-drawn carriages were not an unusual sight in 1933. The Hall building on the left, once a furniture store, now houses Nan Patrick's. The Miss Burlington Diner, a popular eating spot, is on the right. Just beyond the diner is the headquarters of Burlington Light & Power.

The Woman's Christian Temperance Union Temple (WCTU) was formerly the Church of the Berean Baptist Society. The WCTU purchased the property at the northwest corner of South Winooski Avenue on March 31, 1896. The building was torn down in 1950 to erect a gas station.

Looking east on Main Street during the 1920s, the Van Ness House is on the right, with the American Hotel just beyond it. Huge elms on the left denote City Hall Park. Gas stations dotted the city.

The bus terminal at the corner of Main and St. Paul Streets provided ticket service for the railroads as well; they offered special connections that combined bus with rail travel. This photograph was taken in 1930.

This rendering of city hall by the famous New York architectural firm of McKim, Mead, & White shows the winning design selected by Mayor Clarence Beecher and Professor and Dean of the UVM Engineering College J.W. Votey. William M. Kendall, senior partner of McKim, Mead, and White, personally supervised the job.

The Strong Theatre opened on October 24, 1904. Touted as being "practically fireproof" in *About Burlington Vermont*, the building burned in 1970. After years of remaining empty, Court House Square was built on the site. Rubble from the Strong Theatre was used as fill for the bike path located south of Maple Street near Round House Point.

Considered a sign of prosperity during the early part of the century, billboards are no longer seen in Vermont. In this photograph, taken looking south from the intersection of Main Street and South Winooski Avenue, the Strong Theatre is on the right. A gas station is now on the southeast corner; Courthouse Square is on the southwest.

Built by the Public Works Administration (PWA) during the 1930s, the Burlington Street Department is located on Pine Street. The National Industrial Recovery Act was created June 16, 1933, establishing the National Recovery Administration and the Public Works Administration. Providing work for those suffering from the Depression, the PWA completed many civic construction projects across the nation.

Many landmarks are visible in this 1950s aerial view of Burlington. Facing north, the streets, from left to right, are St. Paul, Church, and South Winooski Avenue. Main Street runs from west to east, with City Hall Park and city hall on the left, the post office, courthouse, and Strong Theatre in the center foreground, and the Memorial Auditorium and the Congregational church on the right.

With a new bus in the background, popular WJOY radio personality Val Carter interviews dignitaries from Vermont Transit in front of the bus terminal on St. Paul Street. The turret of the Burlington Savings Bank can be seen in the background.

Four

STREET SCENES

In 1846, the view from what is now Williams Street shows the concentration of Burlington's development closer to the waterfront. Main Street (on the left) was once known as Williston Turnpike.

Built by Abram Stevens and John Johnson for Thaddeus Tuttle in 1804, Grasse Mount encompassed 80 acres. Tuttle purchased the land from Silas Hathaway, who had acquired it from Ira Allen through suspect means. Allen contended that it was Tuttle who had swindled him. Financial reverses forced Tuttle to sell his home to Governor Cornelius Van Ness in 1824.

In 1825, a reception for the Marquis de Lafayette was held at Grasse Mount. Heman Allen, nephew of Ira Allen, rented the mansion from 1829 to 1839, and Mrs. Allen named the house. Ownership changed several times, and the property was eventually divided. Lawrence Barnes bought it in 1866; it was later purchased by Edward Wells, and is now owned by the University of Vermont.

42

Horace Loomis built the house at 342 Pearl Street in 1800. The house served as a social center; famous guests have included Henry Clay and President William Henry Harrison. Elbridge S. Adsit bought the house in 1907 and rented it to the Delta Sigma Society of UVM. After renting the property for 14 years, the Klifa Club, a women's social organization, bought the house. The Klifa Club still owns it.

Fern Hill, the home of John Norton Pomeroy, was located on North Prospect Street. The Ohavi Zedek Synagogue purchased the estate in 1950, built a new synagogue on a portion of the land, and sold the mansion to a fraternity, which abandoned it in 1970. It burned two years later. It is now the site of the Fern Hill Apartments.

This farmhouse, built in 1910 on Colchester Avenue on land owned by the Catholic Diocese, was once called "The Bishop's Orchard." The Sisters of Mercy purchased it in 1918; it served as a home for aged women until 1934. Now known as St. Joseph's Villa, the building is a residence for teachers at Trinity College.

Buell Street, looking East, Burlington. Vt.

Buell Street was named for the family of Ozias Buell, a prosperous merchant during the early 19th century who owned the land extending along Pearl Street from Willard almost to College Street. Ozias' granddaughter Maria married the Rev. Edward Hungerford, who divided the property into building lots and named the resulting streets after the two families.

Retired Rev. John H. Hopkins, Vermont's first Episcopal bishop, was responsible for the acquisition of Rock Point as the educational and administrative center of the diocese. Opened in 1860 as a boys' school and theological center, it later served as a military academy.

Its impressive Gothic architecture covered with vines, Rock Point Institute closed as a military academy in 1899. The building was used for conferences and retreats until it was destroyed by fire in 1979. It was located on Institute Road off North Avenue.

Technically not within the city limits, but comprising an important part of its history, Queen City Park was purchased in 1882 by the Forest City Park Association as a summer resort and for spiritualist camp meetings. Visitors could reach the park via trolley, railroad, and the steamer *Reindeer*, which also made regular stops.

Courting couples enjoyed serene walks along Lovers Lane in Queen City Park for many years. A hotel was built on the grounds that, in 1896, had a capacity of 200. Rooms cost from 50¢ to $1 per day. For $10, a guest could rent a room and eat three meals a day in the dining room for an entire week.

Cove at Queen City Park, Burlington, Vt.

Many families exited the city during the summer to enjoy camps along the lakefront, a practice that continues in our generation. The park was mainly a summer camp area as late as 1946. An underground water system was later installed; the community now exists year-round.

Water slides, boating, and sandy beaches brought large crowds to Queen City Park during the 1920s. More camps dotted the beach. In addition to water activities, there were clay courts on which to play tennis and regularly held dances at the bandstand. (UVM.)

This view, looking east on Williston Road (Route 2) in 1930, shows how much farmland was covered by later development. The building of Interstate 89 in the 1950s forever changed the landscape, bringing shopping centers, supermarkets, and discount stores, as well as an increase in population.

Route 2 was paved with concrete during the 1930s, making the drive from Burlington to Montpelier considerably easier. Travel commentaries during the period lauded this modern highway, which helped decrease the commuting time between the two cities.

Several studies between 1919 and the mid-1930s showed that some of the community's most prominent leaders owned the shabbiest tenements, such as this one in the North End. Although a centralized system for welfare had been attempted, programs remained fragmented until the late 1960s, when the state developed welfare services.

Street construction at North Street and North Avenue was completed at noon on September 4, 1930. McCaffrey's Sunoco now occupies the corner on the left; the gas station on the right during that period is now the Corner Store.

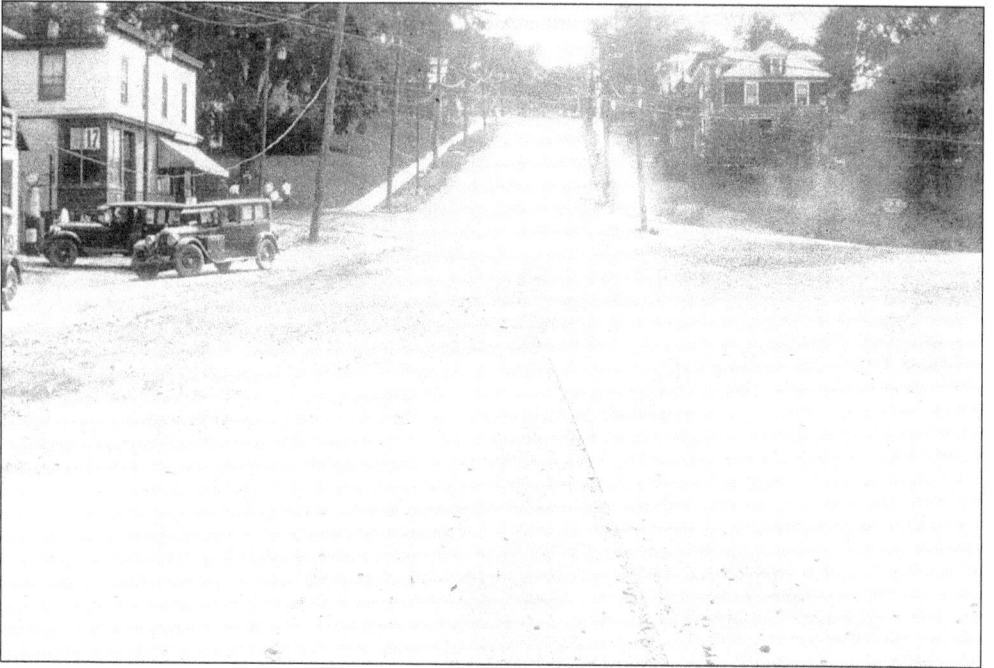

The remnants of trolley tracks remained in the gravel road at the foot of Colchester Avenue near the Winooski Bridge in 1929. The road on the right is Riverside Avenue; beyond the store on the left is Barrett Street.

Once called Star Corner, the rotary is at the five corners where Shelburne Street, Willard Street, St. Paul, Locust Street, and Ledge Road meet. Installed by city engineer George C. Stanley in 1936, the island was designed to slow down traffic.

The Home for Destitute Children was founded in 1865 by Miss Lucia T. Wheeler. Originally a marine hospital built by the government, it was later occupied as a military hospital. Situated on 10 acres on Shelburne Road, the property was purchased in 1866 and renovated at a cost of $30,000.

A portion of the extensive grounds and buildings of the Home for Destitute Children are shown in the lower left of this 1950s aerial photograph. The Grand Union shopping center was newly completed and construction is underway on the building that now houses the Ben Franklin. Highway 189 later followed the ravine on the right.

Looking west, it was not long until the Grand Union shopping center expanded, Highway 189 was constructed, and the Home for Destitute Children had been razed to accommodate a Sears and a supermarket. Home Avenue leads toward Red Rocks; Oak Ledge Park is also visible.

Five

ENTERPRISES

Located at 183 South Champlain Street, Gray's Carriage Manufactory was founded in 1837 by John K. Gray, whose son, Charles B., took over the partnership in 1861 and carried on the business until 1885. The building was converted into apartments in 1885. These Civil War–era customers are looking over available models.

Gray's specialty was phaetons—four-wheeled, lightweight carriages and buggies. His manufactory included a blacksmith shop for ironwork and most probably stables. Though it is not certain whether this is a photograph of the stable at Gray's, it is well kept and shows the respect its owner had for horses.

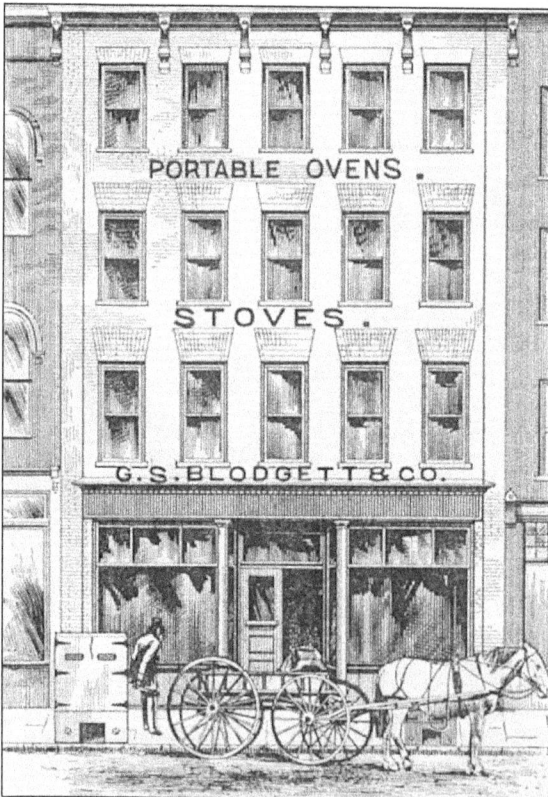

PORTABLE OVENS.

STOVES.

G.S. BLODGETT & CO.

Established in 1854 by Gardner S. Blodgett, G.S. Blodgett & Company built this site on College Street, which the *Burlington Free Press* now occupies. During the 19th century, the company conducted general business as plumbers, steam and gas fitters, and manufacturers of the well-known patent ovens that are still produced at their facility on Lakeside Avenue.

Arbuckle & Company built their candy and cigar factory at 75 Maple Street in 1886. In business since 1870, they were the largest manufacturers of confections in New England outside of Massachusetts. Candy was made in the four-story brick building shown; an adjacent three-story frame building held the cigar factory.

The Wells & Richardson Company, pharmacists and wholesale druggists, were known the world over for Diamond Dyes, Paine's Celery Compound, Lactated Food, Kidney-Wort, and Improved Butter Color. Occupying 58,000 square feet of floor space at 125–133 College Street in 1889, the structures contained the factory, offices, laboratories, printing office, box factory, and photograph gallery.

55

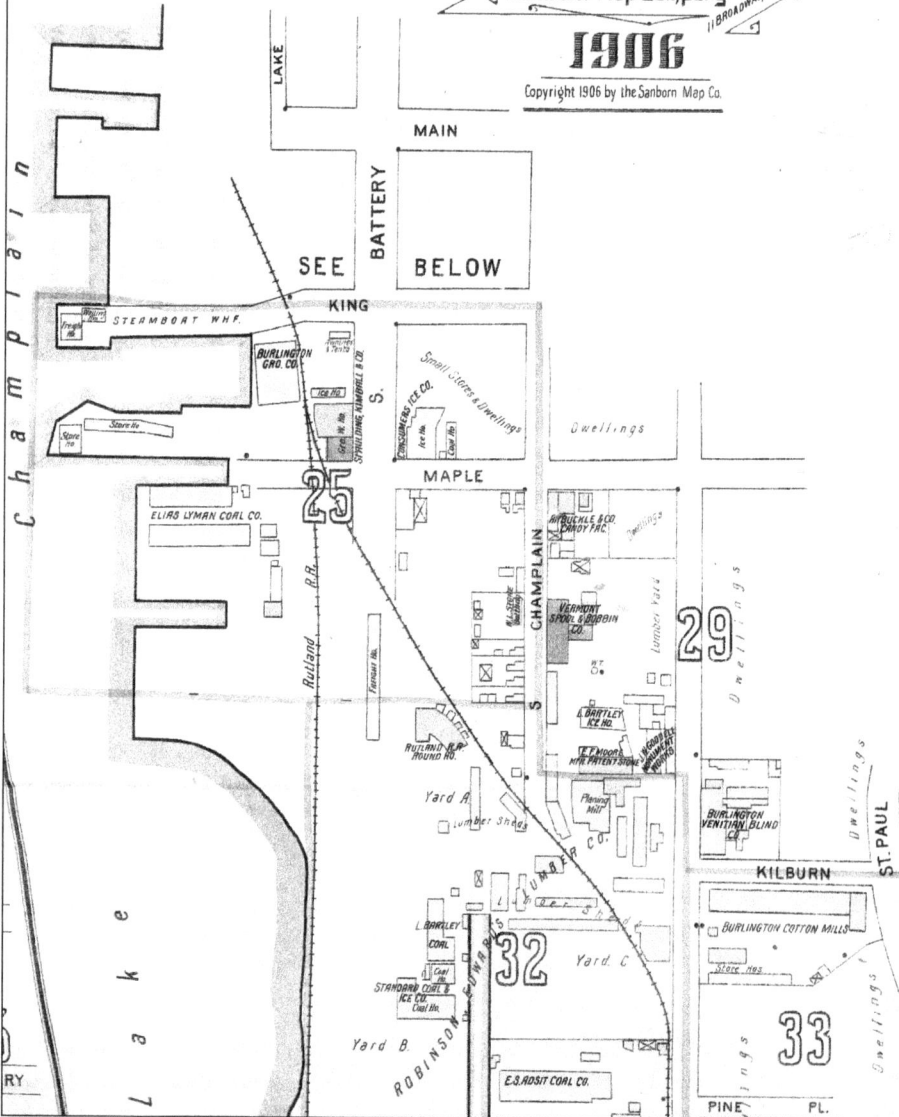

GENERAL MAP of the LUMBER DISTRICT
OF
BURLINGTON
VERMONT

PUBLISHED BY THE Sanborn Map Company 11 BROADWAY, NEW YORK
1906
Copyright 1906 by the Sanborn Map Co.

LAKE

MAIN

BATTERY

SEE BELOW

KING

Champlain

STEAMBOAT WHF.

BURLINGTON GRO. CO.

S. King

SPAULDING, KIMBALL & CO.

ICE HO.

Store Ho.

CONSUMERS ICE CO.

Small Stores & Dwellings

Dwellings

ELIAS LYMAN COAL CO.

MAPLE

Rutland R.R.

ARBUCKLE & CO. CANDY FAC.

S. Champlain

VERMONT SPOOL & BOBBIN CO.

Lumber Yard

29

Dwellings

Lake

Rutland R.R. ROUND HO.

L. BARTLEY ICE HO.

E.T. MOOR'S MFR. PATENT STONE

Yard A

Lumber Sheds

Planing Mill

BURLINGTON VENITIAN BLIND CO.

ST. PAUL

Dwellings

KILBURN

ROBINSON LUMBER CO.

L. BARTLEY COAL

STANDARD COAL & ICE CO. Coal Ho.

32

Yard C

BURLINGTON COTTON MILLS

Store Hos.

Dwellings

33

Yard B

Dwellings

RY

E.S. ADSIT COAL CO.

PINE PL.

Industrial development crept south, following the railroad lines, and a number of manufacturers selected the Pine Street area for their plants. The weaving operation of the Burlington Cotton Mills was on Kilburn Street. Elias Lyman was the treasurer of the Burlington Venetian Blind Company. The J.W. Goodell Monument Company prepared the brownstone used in the YMCA building.

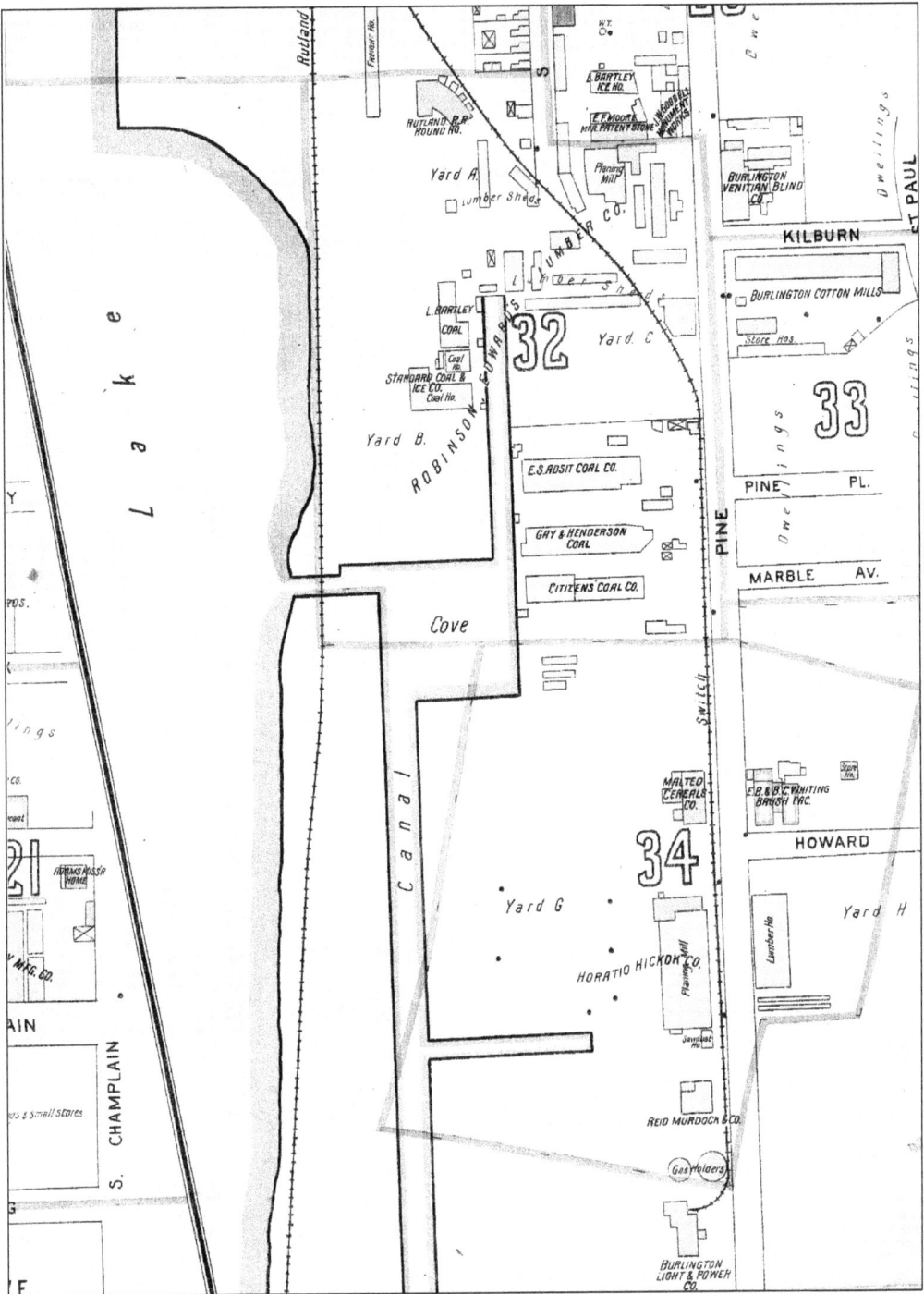

Built in 1900, the Malted Cereals Company factory produced 300 cases of Maltex cereal per day. In the 1950s, "Maypo," a maple-flavored oat cereal, was invented by chemical engineer Herbert A. Bahrenberg. E.B. & A.C. Whiting dressed the fibers used in making brooms and brushes. The Burlington Light & Power Company supplied natural gas for lighting and is now the site of Burlington Electric.

The Queen City Cotton Company once employed 600 people, and was the largest taxpayer in Burlington for many years. Many of the homes in the Lakeside area were built for its employees. The mill's decline began in 1925 and it was dissolved by 1940. After leasing for several years, the Bell Aircraft Corporation purchased the plant in 1946 and sold it to the General Electric Corporation the following year.

Isaac and Abraham Rosenberg deliver groceries with the help of "Teddy." Rosenberg grocers was located at 217 North Street. This 1920 photograph was taken between Washington and Crombie Streets.

George Saiger operated a grocery and dry goods store in the building at 93 North Avenue. This photograph was taken *c.* 1910, after Saiger remodeled the building. Alex Colodny bought the store in 1928, devoted it to groceries, and liquidated the dry goods. The store was successful until Colodny's retirement in 1979. Burlington College now owns the building.

The Cannon Bottling Works was located at 51 Bright Street. Manufacturers of Eagle Brand Sodas, the company was still supplying soft drinks in the 1930s. Like Saiger's Department Store, the owners of the enterprise were an integral part of Burlington's Jewish community.

Before the advent of supermarkets, each neighborhood had a corner grocery similar to the one at Intervale and Riverside Avenues. Photographed in 1930, this may be the store owned by Sophia Saiger.

Mazel's Clothing Store was a fixture on North Avenue for many years. This 1930 photograph also shows the Silver Star Restaurant, which was owned by Abraham Solomon, and one of the early Grand Unions that opened in the city.

F.W. Woolworth, located on the corner of Church and Cherry Streets, was the largest store of the chain in New England during the 1940s. The company went bankrupt in the late 1990s. The building was torn down for the construction of the Burlington Square Mall.

Also located on Church Street, Kresge's offered the 1940 shopper a variety of household goods, clothing, do-it-yourself equipment, and personal care items. As a child, it was fun to browse the counters, where merchandise was more accessible, easy to locate, and often cost less than a quarter.

The Coca-Cola Bottling Plant at 266 Pine was built by Kieslich Construction. This 1948 photograph shows the fleet of trucks owned by the firm. After the bottling company moved elsewhere, specialty food manufactures and other businesses occupied the space.

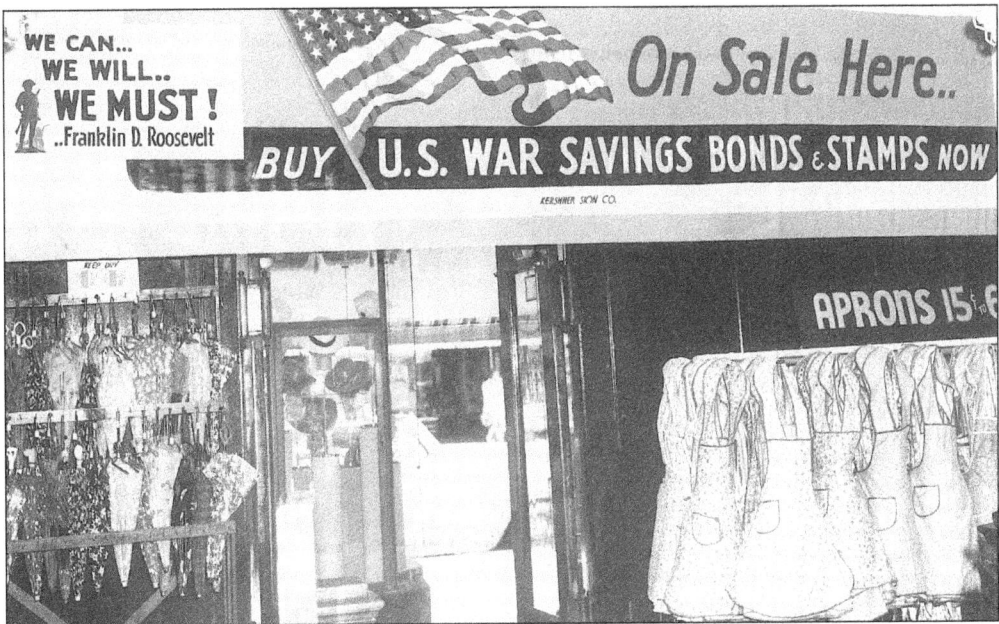

A poster inside Fishman's Department Store on Church Street advertised the sale of War Bonds, which helped finance defense efforts during World War II. Although aprons could be purchased for as little as 15¢, silk stockings were scarce, as silk was diverted to make parachutes. (UVM.)

The Burlington Shoe Repairing Company was situated on Church Street between College and Bank Streets. The c. 1950s theater bills in the window advertise *Bringing Up Baby* and *The Adventures of Tom Sawyer* playing at the Flynn, and *Stolen Heaven* at the Majestic. (UVM.)

Howard Johnson's on Shelburne Road was popular spot for family dining during the late 1950s. Advertisements for the restaurant emphasized that it was on the South End bus line. Closed in the late 1980s, the restaurant became the Panda Inn, specializing in Chinese food.

William R. Hauke, building contractor, constructed the shopping center on North Avenue. The Grand Union is still in the same location. A bank is in the corner space on the right, and Ben Franklin later moved into a second building erected adjacent to this one.

Six

CELEBRATING CHAMPLAIN

Samuel de Champlain first sailed onto Lake Champlain on July 4, 1609. Communities situated along the lake from Swanton to Vergennes celebrated the event in 1909 with carefully coordinated festivities that lasted a full week. This representation shows Champlain's ship, the *Don de Dieu*, moored in Burlington Harbor.

American, French, and Canadian flags line Church Street, crisscrossed with electric bulbs used for special night illumination. The Rev. William C. Gordon of Boston wrote in the *Christian Endeavor World* that the crowd was orderly and well behaved, and that no robbery or theft was reported to the police during the celebration.

Historic pageants were presented on a floating island 300 feet in length. The island carried its own power and electric lights; it was said that the night performances looked more realistic than those held in daylight. The actors were 175 lineal descendants of members of the Iroquois Confederacy. Sarro Tso Ni Te, a Mohawk Indian, played Hiawatha.

This picture was taken Thursday, July 8, from a corner of the floating stage. A depiction of Champlain's battle with the Native Americans and the drama *Hiawatha* were performed. Single tickets for the Thursday performance cost $1.50 for the choicest seats. Season tickets for the eight events cost $4.

Members of the 11th U.S. Cavalry from Fort Ethan Allen participated in Thursday's "Great Military Parade" up Church Street. Other military groups included regiments from Vermont and New York, the governor-general's Foot-Guards from Ottawa, Canada, and Armstrong's Algonquins from Upper Canada.

Made up of representatives from all schools in the Montpelier School District, the Montpelier Fife and Drum Corps of 75 schoolboys was said to be the largest such group in the world. The parade was reviewed by the presidential party, foreign guests, and state and local dignitaries.

Electric lights illuminated Church Street in a manner never before attempted. This photograph was probably taken quite late, after the revelers had returned to their lodgings.

An hour late, President William Howard Taft arrived in Burlington on the steamer *Ticonderoga*, which tied up at the Champlain Yacht Club. A 21-gun salute was fired as Taft stepped ashore; Canadian boats in the harbor dipped their flags in salute.

Speeches were held in City Hall Park with Governor G.H. Prouty presiding. President Taft's address was well received, as were those of Ambassador Jusserand of France (shown speaking in the central photograph), Ambassador Bryce of England, Governor Charles Hughes of New York, Mayor James Burke, and others.

It was estimated that 60,000 people attended the Burlington celebration on July 8. It was standing room only in City Hall Park as thousands flowed onto the adjacent streets in an attempt to hear the President's speech.

Charles E. Allen (left), Mayor James E. Burke (center), and Walter J. Bigelow were instrumental in putting together the Burlington celebration. A great success for the city and the state, the Boston *Zion's Herald* stated, "On the whole, it was a memorable tercentenary, and observed with remarkable enthusiasm."

71

Members of the Tercentenary Commission included Walter H. Crockett of Montpelier; John M. Thomas of Middlebury; Horace W. Bailey of Newbury; Lynn M. Hays of Essex Junction, secretary; George H. Prouty of Newport, chairman; Frank L. Fish of Vergennes, treasurer; Arthur F. Stone of St. Johnsbury; William J. VanPatten of Burlington; F.O. Beaupre of Burlington; and George T. Jarvis of Rutland.

Seven

HAPPENINGS

Although professional theatrical groups brought music, opera, and plays to Burlington, local groups performed in their own productions for entertainment. Musical and literary events were quite popular and Burlington's organizations each presented at least one such event yearly. (UVM.)

Centennial Field was used for a myriad of sporting events: baseball, football, and track and field. Shown *c.* 1910, these gentlemen are cheering runners across the finish line. A marathon race of 26 miles and 385 yards was run on this field during the tercentenary celebration; Patrick Dineen won the race in three hours. (UVM.)

Troops trained at the University of Vermont during World War I. The training benefited the military and brought revenue to the university and the community. In 1918, Company B, U.S.

The Burlington Traction Company was given authority to run buses in 1926, but continued trolley service until 1929. Crowds at Main and St. Paul Streets in 1929 watch the symbolic burning of a trolley car, which marked the end of one era of transport and the beginning of another. (UVM.)

Army Training Detachment at the University of Vermont, was commanded by Lt. Charles Austin. The photograph was taken in front of Morrill Hall.

Chittenden County 4H leaders and members gather during the 1930s at Memorial Auditorium for their annual meeting and awards ceremonies. Margaret Poole McDonough is third from

Jack Dempsey, former world-heavyweight boxing champ, refereed the wrestling main event at Memorial Auditorium between Don Eagle and Henry (Blond Bomber) Kulkavitch on November 27, 1945. Kulkavitch got out of hand, and Dempsey flattened him with a right to the jaw, awarding the bout to Eagle. Dempsey (center) is shown relaxing with friends afterwards. (UVM.)

left in the top row. The organization has long taught husbandry, homemaking, gardening, and farming skills to millions of children throughout the country.

J.C. Penney's moved to the street level of the New Sherwood Hotel in 1928, followed by Sears, Roebuck & Company in 1938. When fire destroyed the building in 1940, the flames and smoke could be seen for miles.

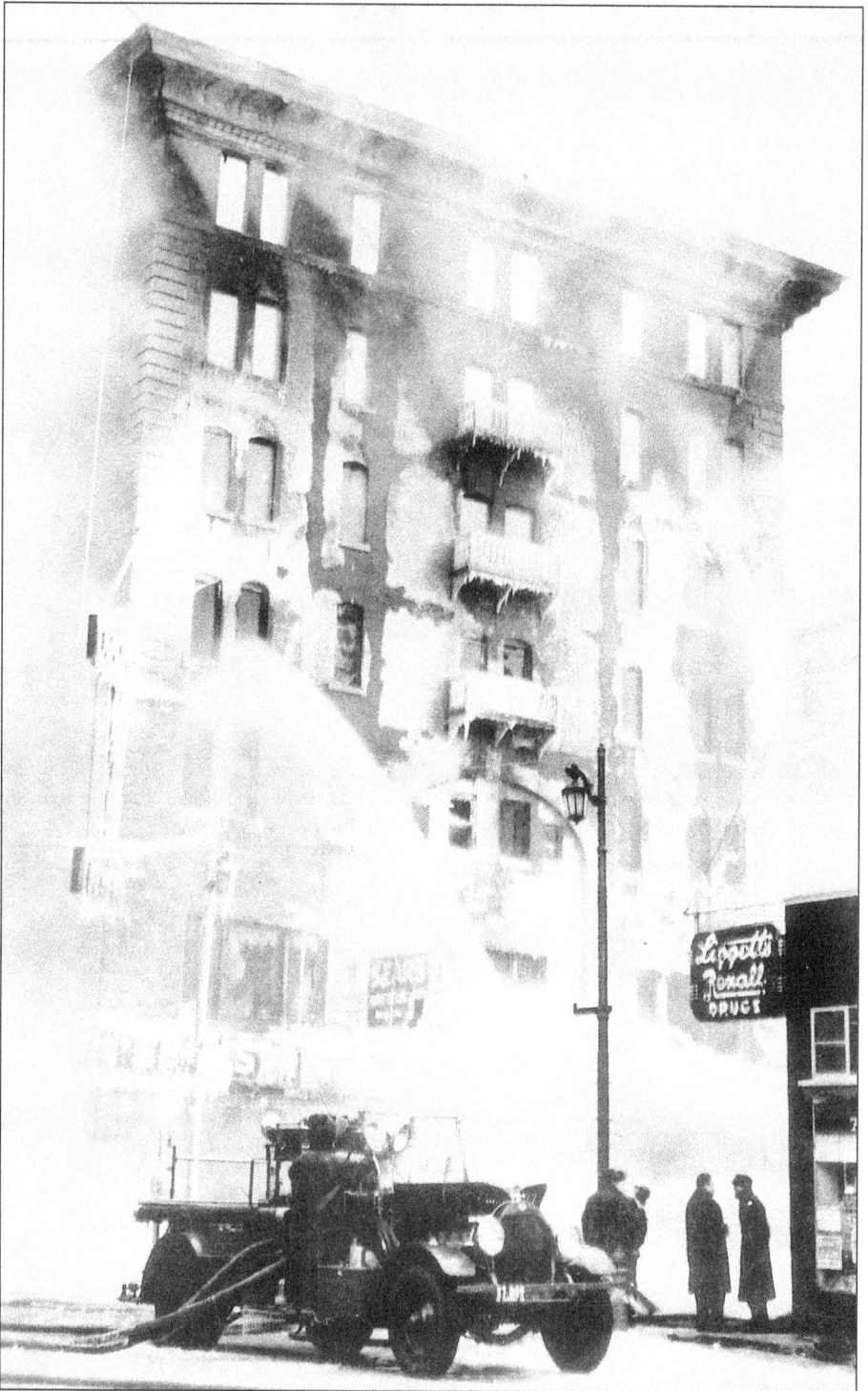

Icicles formed as streams of water extinguished the last of the flames. A new building was built to house J.C. Penney's and Sears in 1941. J.C. Penney's took over the entire building in 1964, when Sears moved to the Shelburne Road Plaza. (UVM.)

A procession of Trinity College students carried the statue of Our Lady of Fatima to Winooski, where students from St. Michael's College picked it up. The statue was carried across the nation as a symbol of peace and faith during the mid-1950s.

Vermont has produced a Miss United States of America! Photographed in the fall of 1954, from left to right, are Nancy Allen Epping, Miss New Hampshire; Annabelle Katherine Pinkham, Miss Vermont; and Carlene Johnson, Miss United States of America and the former Miss Vermont.

Annabelle Pinkham (center) is shown with employees of WDOT after her selection as Miss Vermont. Vin d'Acuti is on the right. Approximately 1,000 persons attended the pageant and ball at Memorial Auditorium.

Eight

THE MOODY WINOOSKI

The Winooski River has many moods, from gentle benefactor to raging tyrant. Shown at flood stage on November 24, 1927, the torrent washed away buildings and heavily damaged the mills. Rivers throughout Vermont flooded, causing 84 deaths and property losses of approximately $30 million statewide, affecting 18,880 individuals.

The Winooski River has been known to overflow its banks many times, whether from ice jams, snow melting, or heavy rains. Floodwaters, as in this 1880s photograph of the Winooski Valley, deposit nutrient-laden silt that enriches the farmland.

A wooden bridge, which traversed the Winooski Gorge during the 19th century, was later replaced by a two-span steel railway bridge. The force of the floodwaters tore the 250-ton bridge from its foundations and washed it downstream for a quarter of a mile, dropping it on an island.

During the 1890s, the intersection of Prospect Street and Riverside Avenue gave an unbroken view of the river. This photograph was taken from Fern Hill.

A covered bridge spanned the river between Burlington and Winooski during the time of the Civil War. Waters flowed swiftly through Salmon Hole (pictured above); the area was as well known for fishing then as it is now. The building on the right is the Johnson Grain Mill.

This 1900 view shows a more modern bridge and an expansion of the mills on the Winooski side of the river. Years later, during the 1927 flood, the Johnson Grain Company was dynamited to provide another channel for the floodwaters and prevent further damage to the mills.

Ira Allen once operated a mill on the site of the Chace Mill. Known as the "Cotton Factory" before the Civil War, it became the Burlington Cotton Mills in 1868. Chace Mills of Fall River, Massachusetts, purchased the firm in 1906, about the time of this photograph. It now serves as office and studio space.

The Winooski Bridge was torn from its abutments, the remnants of which are shown in this snapshot taken a few days after the 1927 Flood. Hundreds of men frantically tried to save the structure, but the constant pounding of wreckage caused it to break apart, severing the link between Winooski and Burlington.

Rock outcroppings in the Salmon Hole were reshaped by the flood and the dynamiting of the Johnson Grain Company. A small portion of the building's foundation is visible on the right. Some of the foundation can still be seen today.

Only foot traffic was allowed on the pontoon bridge that provided temporary access between Burlington and Winooski. It was built and maintained by the military, including the Seventh Field Artillery and Third Cavalry Regiments from Fort Ethan Allen, until the permanent bridge was completed in 1928.

An aerial view shows the new bridge under construction and the pontoon bridge in use. Restoration started statewide immediately after the waters subsided. By February 1, 1928, 14,510 persons in the flood areas of the state had been aided. It was a large undertaking, for 300 buildings had been destroyed and 1,247 had been damaged in Vermont alone.

Nine

SCHOOL DAYS

In the 1930s, these Burlington schoolchildren were costumed for a pageant depicting other nations. As in most school pageants, the enthusiasm of the participants varies.

Located on the east side of South Union Street between Bay View and Howard Streets, the Adams School was built in 1902 on the site of an older school building that had been erected in 1874. It remained in use until the late 1970s and has been converted into office space for private companies.

Built on the site of a Baptist French Mission chapel, the Archibald Street School stands on the corner of Archibald and Spring Streets. The site was purchased in 1888. The brick structure shown was built in 1905 and accommodated five teachers and 140 students.

The Lawrence Barnes School occupies the site of the old "North and Murray School." The lot was originally purchased May 1, 1854. The building shown was first occupied in 1896 and cost about $30,000 to build. The 1905 school census showed 11 teachers and 360 pupils.

The S.W. Thayer School was built in 1894 on the site of a former schoolhouse that had been in use since before the Civil War. The building still stands next to the state offices on North Avenue and houses a retail pharmacy and other offices.

School assembly or a music lesson? No one is certain, but the audience is paying attention as Val Carter of WJOY (at the piano) and an accordionist entertain students at one of the area schools during the early 1950s.

When Christ the King opened in 1939, the building contained a church on the ground floor, with nine classrooms on the second and third floors. A two-story annex was built in 1961. Located on the corner of Locust and Shelburne Streets, the lot was once the orchard of the Hickok Estate.

St. Anthony's school was built on Pine Street behind St. Anthony's Church in 1931. This 1950s photograph shows a group of schoolboys in front. The school closed in 1971 and was torn down in 1980.

Located at Rock Point, Bishop Hopkins Hall opened in 1888 as a finishing school for girls, but it failed financially and closed in 1899. It reopened in 1928, again as a girl's boarding school, but designed to meet the needs of those with difficulties. It is now Rock Point School.

The main entrance of Cathedral High School faced Pearl Street with a side entrance on St. Paul. The Cathedral of the Immaculate Conception is to the left. In 1922, the streets in Burlington were not yet paved.

The class of 1922 poses in front of Cathedral High School. Graduates were facing a life much different from their parents. Automobile, telephones, and electricity were commonplace; radio and moving pictures brought information much more quickly; and the Nineteenth Amendment, which provided for women's suffrage, was unanimously declared constitutional by the U.S. Supreme Court.

Most high school business departments had a "commercial room" devoted to the instruction of business-related subjects. Students' accounts at the Cathedral High School Bank taught them money management. Today's students would bemoan the absence of calculators.

The typing classroom contained the most up-to-date Royal typewriters of the time. Teachers ensured their pupils maintained proper posture and hand position. Accuracy was a large determinant of success. Fifty words per minute with no mistakes was much more acceptable than 75 with five or more errors.

Cathedral's 1922 basketball team soundly trounced its opponents and emerged as Vermont State Champions. Seen here, from left to right, are as follows: (front row) Perrotta, Boiselle, Polworth, and Crosby; (back row) McGaughan, Stannard, Coach Hammond, Cassell, and Gervais.

The 1922 varsity squad of Cathedral High School shows that basketball uniforms have not greatly changed over the years—although, instead of knee braces, many players now wear kneepads.

A pool and bowling academy also provided recreation for Cathedral High students. Sports played an important part in the physical education routine.

The varsity baseball team of Burlington High School ended the 1956 season second in the Northern League. Coach Orrie Jay is fourth from the right in the top row; Ray Pecor is first on the left in the second row. Orrie Jay Field on North Avenue was named after the high school's favorite coach.

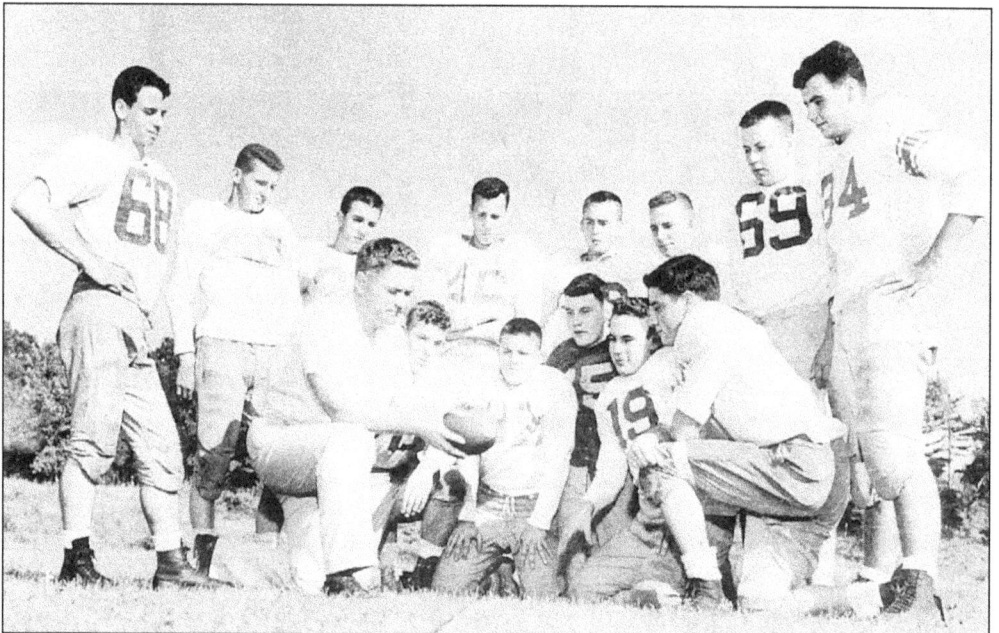

Burlington High has always been known for its varsity football teams. The 1956 season was one of the most difficult the Seahorses faced; many injured players weakened the team. Coach Adams is holding the ball.

Called the "Sea Lassies," the girl's basketball team showed notable improvement over the winter. Mariska Stades, an exchange student from Holland (third from left in the second row), played on the 1956–57 team. That same year the Sea Lassies played in Canada, at Stanstead, Quebec, for the first time.

Another important part of the high school sports scene was the majorettes. The 1956–57 Burlington High School Twirling Corps included, from left to right, Donna Witham, Louise Schimmelpfennig, Elizabeth Nuquist, Jean McAllister, Mrs. Jobling (adviser), Janet Bruhn, Joan Murphy, and Jean Fuller.

Students enter Burlington High School at the corner of Main and South Union Streets in the winter of 1957. The site is now Edmunds Middle School. Then, as now, high school students did not consider wearing hats and gloves "cool."

Ten

ON THE HILL

The canopies of trees that graced University Row and the Green had not yet succumbed to Dutch Elm disease in the 1940s. Chartered in 1791 and rechartered in 1865 as the University of Vermont and State Agricultural College, UVM became the first land-grant university in the United States.

Morrill Hall, "The Old Mill," Williams Science Hall, Billings Library, and the Ira Allen Chapel stand out in this c. 1930 aerial view of UVM. The buildings were often photographed at the turn of the century. A number of photographs from 1909 follow in this chapter.

During 1905, the Old Mill was the main college building on campus. This structure, which was built in three sections, replaced the original college, which burned in 1824. General Lafayette laid the cornerstone of the south wing in 1825. The remodeling in 1882 softened the severity of its facade, which had prompted its nickname.

Designed by acclaimed architect Henry Hobson Richardson, Billings Library was completed in 1885. Funds for the building were donated by Frederick Billings, a UVM alumnus and president of the Northern Pacific Railway. No longer a library, Billings was renovated into a student center in 1963.

Constructed in 1896 and donated by Dr. Edward H. Williams, Williams Science Hall was said to be the first fireproof building in the nation. Converted to an art building during the latter half of this century, its art gallery was dedicated to the memory of art professor and artist Francis Colburn in 1977.

The Boulder Society of the class of 1909 stands behind the UVM boulder in front of the Old Mill. Seniors formed the honor society in 1905. The almost-perfect sphere was naturally formed. It was donated to the university in 1849 by former governor Charles Paine, president of the Vermont Central Railroad.

John Heman Converse donated the hall that bears his name. Located near the Given Medical Building, the dormitory was once reserved for freshmen. A UVM graduate, Converse donated funds for several buildings, including the gymnasium shown below.

Designed by Andrews, Jacques, and Rantoulin in 1901, the campus gymnasium is shown here c. 1909. An extension was added in 1915. It was converted into classrooms and offices in 1963. The building was renovated into a 291-seat theater named for Royall Tyler, who is considered America's first important playwright.

The 1909 "Ariel" board put together the UVM yearbook. Women who worked on the publication were Miss Ethel Pearl Southwick of Burlington (on the left) and Miss Mary Robinson (on the right). Mr. Mulcare, editor-in-chief, is seated in the center.

A group of 1909 seniors poses on the steps in front of Billings Library. As was the custom of the time, none of the female members of the class are included in the photograph. The ornate moldings surrounding the arch were carved by Alexander Miln.

Whether 1909 or 1999, graduation caps and gowns have not changed. In addition to the commencement exercises, the celebrants enjoyed a promenade and boat ride. Note that the women graduates were included in this photograph, unlike the previous one.

At Trinity College, academic gowns were not worn for commencement alone; in 1937, members of the Sodality Club wore them daily to mass and all campus affairs. The purpose of the Sodality Club was to honor the Blessed Virgin and grow spiritually in service to others.

The 1887 graduating class of the UVM Medical School sits in front of the old Medical College. Originally a two-story building constructed in 1829, an additional story and the entrance tower were added in 1858. The building was named Pomeroy Hall in honor of Dr. John Pomeroy, founder of the Medical School.

Photographed in 1899, medical students stand in front of the old Medical School. At this time, Pomeroy Hall held the Agricultural Experiment Station, as well as dormitory rooms for agricultural students on the third floor. Alternately used by the speech and communications departments, the building now houses classrooms and studios for UVM Media Services.

106

Well respected, but said to be severe with students, Dr. William Darling was a professor of Anatomy from 1872 to 1884. It is said that when angered, he would lapse into a broad Scots accent. Because of this, he was often the brunt of student pranks.

Ashbel Parmelee Grinnell became dean of the College of Medicine in 1874 and served until 1877; after a hiatus, he served in the same position from 1882 to 1898. Grinnell had considerable influence; under his leadership the faculty remained stable and the school experienced prosperity. He stepped down when the Medical School came under full control of the university.

The new Medical College was built in 1884 at the corner of Pearl and Prospect Streets. A rift occurred between the university trustees and the medical faculty in 1899. By 1909, when this photograph was taken, the trustees had taken full control and management of the Medical Department. They had also voted to provide an annual salary of $1,200 to the faculty professors.

Eleven

COMMUNITY MEDICINE

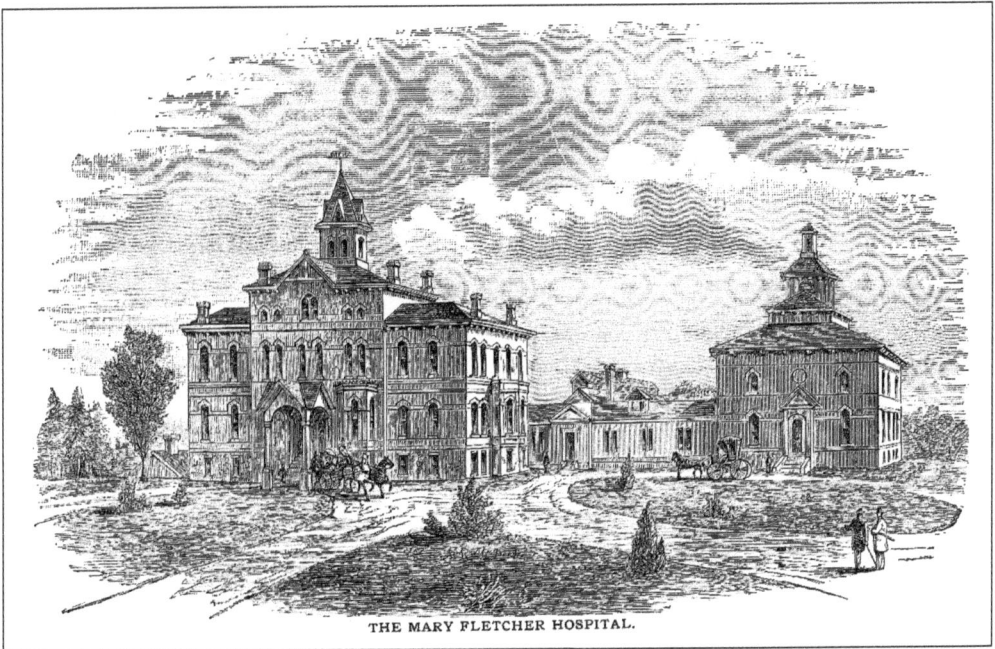

THE MARY FLETCHER HOSPITAL.

Chartered by the state legislature in 1876, the Mary Fletcher Hospital opened for patients in 1879. Hospital buildings were added in 1887, including a women's ward, an isolated ward for severe surgical cases, and a building containing a room for the preparation of surgical dressings and an operating room. In 1889, the hospital had 43 beds, and could accommodate 50 in an emergency.

In operation since 1883, Dr. Sparhawk's Sanitarium moved into new quarters at 150 Bank Street in June of 1887. The smaller building on the left contained an electro vapor bath, where Turkish, Russian, and combined baths were given "to suit the needs of both sick and well."

Several sanitariums were in operation in Burlington during the late 19th century. Most of them treated nervous disorders or mental illness and were designed to provide a quiet environment for the patients. Located on Shelburne Road, the Green Mountain Sanatorium was said to be "comfortable and restful."

When the Mary Fletcher Hospital opened in 1879, a student at the School of Nursing could graduate in four weeks. By 1941, nursing candidates were required to complete three years of work and study. These student nurses have just received their caps at the Florence Nightingale Candlelight Ceremony.

Dr. Frank Ober, a visiting professor of orthopedic surgery from Harvard Medical College, conducted an orthopedic clinic at the hospital. Students in the gallery observed him as he examined a patient. In addition to those problems caused by accidents and birth defects, many children's orthopedic problems were caused by polio.

Young patients convalesce in a bright, sunny area of the original hospital building. The room seems rather spartan compared to the playroom on today's pediatric floor.

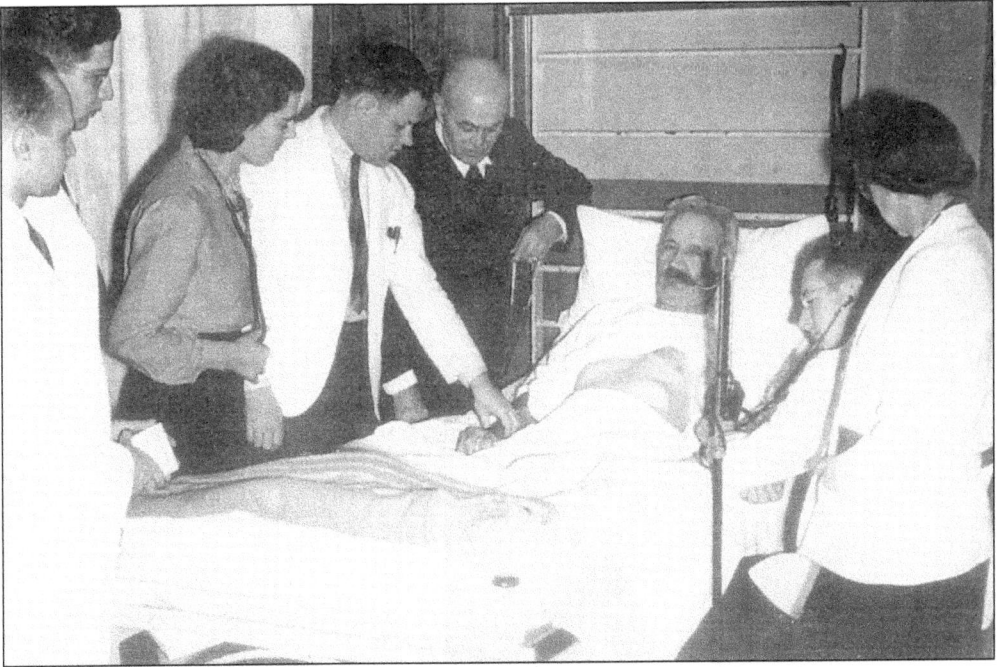

Primarily a teaching hospital in 1940, as it is today, students accompany a physician on patient rounds. With the exception of Yale, the Mary Fletcher Hospital was the only New England institution outside of Boston to provide an "A" medical education rating at that time.

The amphitheater allowed each student an unobstructed view of the professor. This class was learning diagnosis and watched the demonstration of techniques closely as Dr. C.H. Beecher lectured.

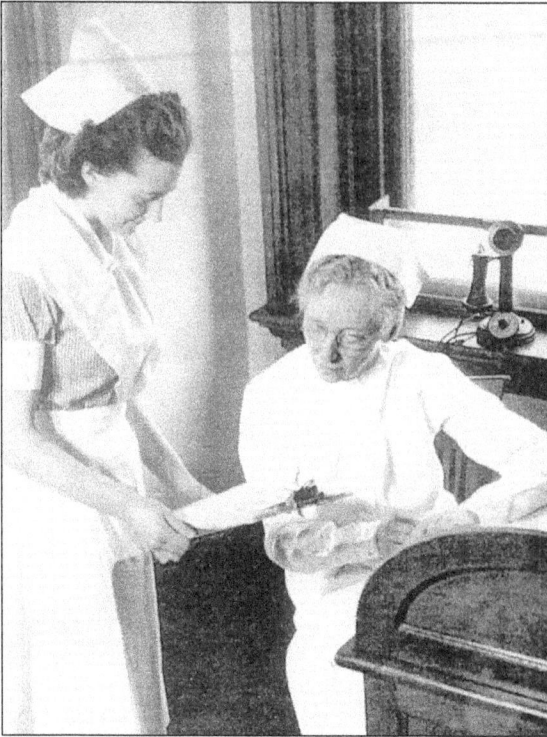

Nursing students made regular reports on the patients they were caring for and the other work they were doing. Here Alma B. van Pelt, RN director of the nursing school, receives a student's report.

In addition to provisions purchased by the hospital, the hospital also accepted donations of home-canned foods for patient meals. A nurse supervises a kitchen worker in this 1940s photograph.

The equipment for administering a basal metabolism test seems primitive to today's observer. During this period, space was at a premium; a women's ward was added in 1941. Plans for new laboratory, x-ray, surgical, and physical therapy facilities were underway.

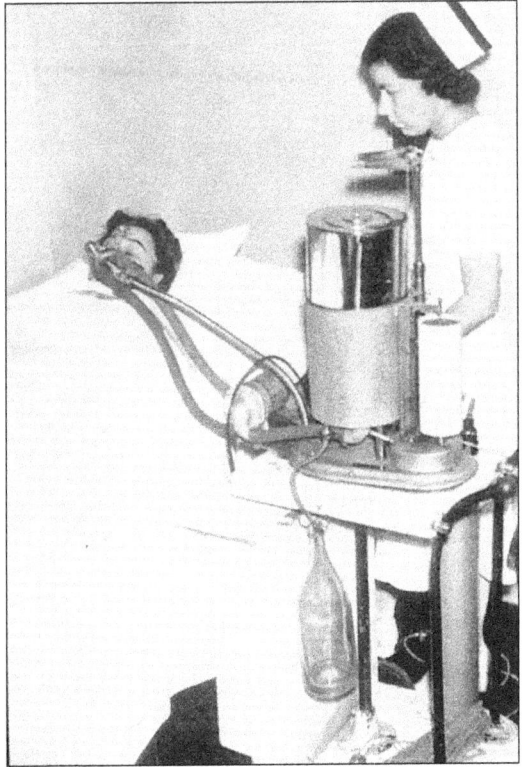

Fletcher's x-ray department was approved for diagnostic and therapeutic work by the American College of Surgeons and the National Cancer Institute. A forerunner of radiation treatment, this nurse is using the "deep X-ray machine" in an attempt to kill cancer cells.

The 1941 Board of Directors of the Mary Fletcher Hospital included prominent Burlington citizens. Seen here, from left to right, are Guy M. Page, Frederick W. Shepardson, E.E. Clarkson, Roy L. Patrick, Dr. Thomas S. Brown, Dr. H.A. Kemp, and M.C. Grandy.

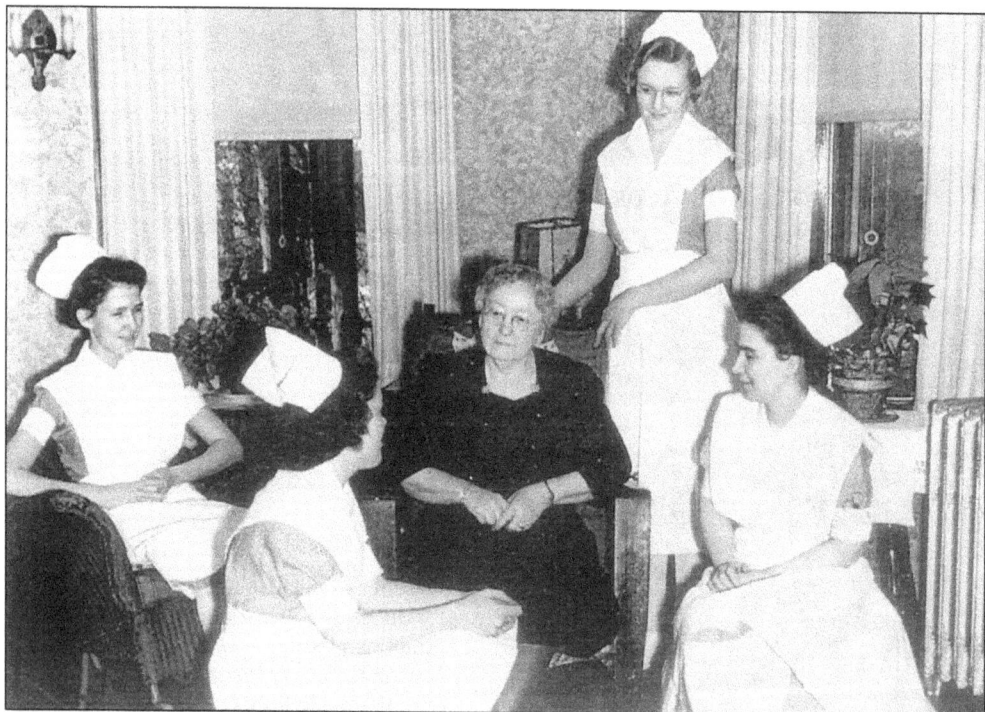

Nursing students lived in the Nurses Home, which was part of the hospital. Mrs. White, the housemother, not only supervised her charges, she was often their confidante and adviser.

Twelve

NEIGHBORING FAITHS

Between 1885 and 1940, the Old North End was home to Burlington's Jewish community. Known locally as "Little Jerusalem," Jews primarily from Lithuania preserved their small-town, Eastern European culture. A 1915 procession from the Ahavath Gerim Synagogue to the Hebrew Free School passes the Star Creamery in this photograph.

"IN THE YEAR 5645 OF THE ERA OF CREATION (1885 C.E.) (1816 YEARS AFTER THEIR EXILE AND WANDERING) ABOUT EIGHTEEN PEOPLE, EXILES OF RUSSIA GATHERED HERE IN THE CITY OF BURLINGTON, THE FIRST CONGREGATION IN [BURLINGTON,] VERMONT. AND HERE ALSO, BEFORE THEY WERE SETTLED, THEY THOUGHT OF FOUNDING A HOUSE OF PRAYER FOR THEIR TORAH AND THEIR FAITH. THEY KEPT THEIR CHARGE."

HARRIS W. SACKS, MARCH 30, 1908 (CANTOR 1892-1922, RABBI 1922-1925)

AHAVATH GERIM SYNAGOGUE: "LOVE OF STRANGERS"
1909-1937
142 ARCHIBALD STREET

OHAVI ZEDEK SYNAGOGUE: "LOVERS OF JUSTICE"
1885-1952
168 ARCHIBALD STREET

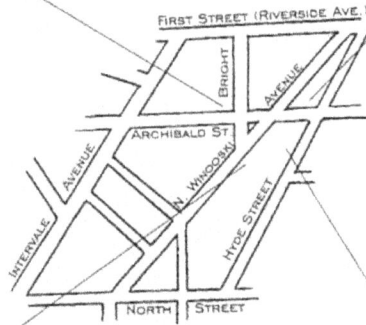

FIRST STREET (RIVERSIDE AVE.)

BRIGHT AVENUE

ARCHIBALD ST.

INTERVALE AVENUE

N. WINOOSKI STREET

HYDE STREET

NORTH STREET

TALMUD TORAH: HEBREW FREE SCHOOL
1910-1952
264 NORTH WINOOSKI AVENUE

CHAI ADAM SYNAGOGUE: "LIFE OF MAN"
1889-1939
105 HYDE STREET

This plaque commemorates the establishment of the Jewish community and shows the location of the synagogues and the Hebrew Free School.

118

In this c. 1903 photograph, one can see a Simhat Torah, the festival that celebrates the conclusion of the annual reading cycle of the Torah, at the Ohavi Zedek Synagogue. From a small community numbering 150 in 1890, it had increased to 700 residents in 1910. By the 1930s, more than 1,100 Jews lived in Little Jerusalem.

The procession left from the Ahavath Gerim Synagogue to the Talmud Torah, or the Hebrew Free School, in 1915. The house at 142 Archibald Street was purchased from Dr. Sam Sparhawk in 1907 and remodeled into a synagogue that was used for worship until 1937. According to city records, the building became a Baptist church in 1946.

Members of Bethel Lodge #22 of the Knights of Pythias celebrate their 13th anniversary. A fraternal organization for Jewish men, the lodge was organized on March 8, 1900.

The interior of Ohavi Zedek in 1910 shows the hexagonal-shaped Bimah (a raised platform with a reading desk from which the liturgy is led) in the foreground. In an orthodox synagogue, men are seated on the main floor and women in the gallery.

This closer view shows the holy ark that contains the Torah. Carved tablets depicting the Ten Commandments are between the lions above the ark. Unfortunately, the chandelier obscures them in this photograph.

Ohavi Zedek's congregation purchased the building from a stonecutter who made tombstones for St. Joseph's Cemetery. A new synagogue and community center was built in 1952 on North Prospect Street. A group eventually decided to separate and formed Ahavath Gerim, an orthodox congregation not connected to the old synagogue of the same name.

The Chai Adam Synagogue was built at 105 Hyde Street and dedicated on July 10, 1889. The congregation eventually affiliated with Ohavi Zedek in 1939, but retained possession of the building until 1952. This incredible mural painted by Benzion Black was discovered on the ceiling when the building was being remodeled. It is now a seven-unit apartment house.

Lions flank the Ten Commandments in this close-up of the Benzion Black mural at Chai Adam. A sign painter by trade, Black had a shop at 13 Center Street. This and the preceding mural were photographed by Joel Gardner.

Formed in 1830, the First Baptist Society formally organized in 1834. The society bought the property on St. Paul Street in 1863 and dedicated its new church building on December 15, 1864. In 1905, the group veneered the exterior of the church with brick and installed 12 stained-glass windows. The windows were gifts from the daughters of Mr. and Mrs. C.C. Post.

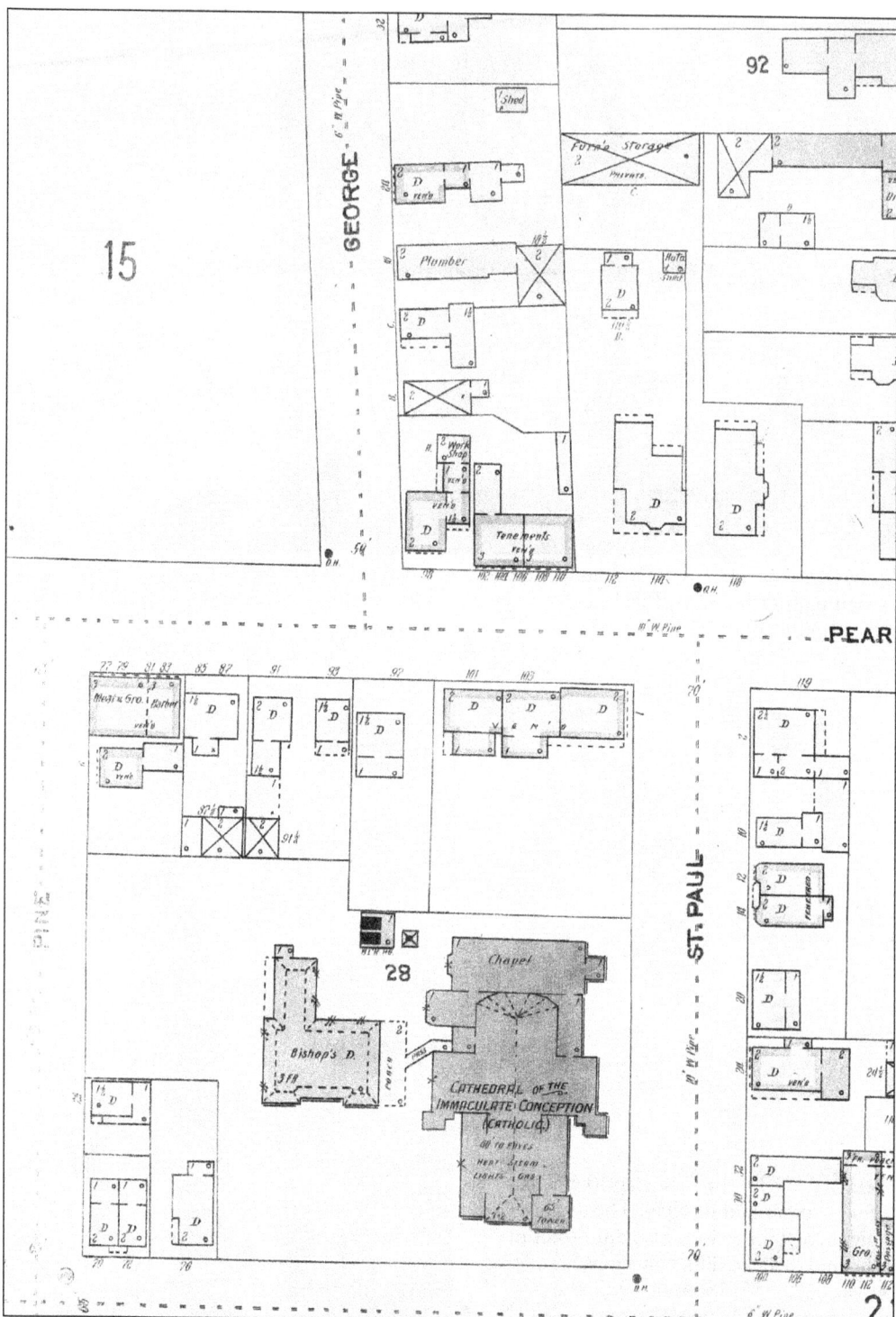

The Cathedral of the Immaculate Conception and the bishop's residence were surrounded by homes during the early part of this century. Built in 1867, the cathedral was destroyed in 1972 in a fire set by a former altar boy.

Completion of the cathedral was stopped by the Civil War, and the main tower remained incomplete until 1904. This photograph was taken *c. 1870*.

Originally the bishop's residence, the cathedral rectory faced Cherry Street. In 1906, a porch on the east side of the structure and a breezeway connected the two buildings.

St. Patrick's Convent was blessed in 1876 and became part of the Cathedral Grammar School. This photograph was taken around 1880.

The Bishop's Throne was on the west side of the cathedral's sanctuary. The throne, bearing Bishop Joyce's coat of arms, was destroyed in the fire.

The shrine of St. Peter's Chains in St. Patrick's Chapel contained a full-size replica of the chain fastened around the neck of St. Peter when he was led to his death. The original is kept in the Basilica of St. Peter in Chains in Rome. The reliquary sitting before the chains is said to have contained a link from the original.

The marble crypt beneath the floor of the cathedral contained the bodies of Bishop DeGoesbriand, Bishop Michaud, and Bishop Rice, from top to bottom on the left.

Founded to serve the French-speaking Catholics in the South End, St. Anthony's Church was built at the corner of Pine and Flynn Streets in 1902. Bricks, stained-glass windows, and the church bell all came from the first St. Joseph's Church on North Prospect Street.

Built in 1941, St. Mark's Parish on North Avenue was the most modern church building in Burlington for at least 20 years. Considered innovative, its architectural design became nationally known and appeared in a textbook on architecture.